12/17

Blessings of
Great Health
Always! 3 John 2

This is a gift from Mother
Beatrice Duke, who
always believed and stood
on the Powerful Words of
God. She Wants the same
for you and God's Words
to Speak! His Words
Always! His Words never
return void!

Isaiah 55:9&11

1

ACKNOWLEDGEMENTS

I wish to express my appreciation to:

Janet Haire

For the hours she spent typing and retyping the manuscript.

Jacquie Rich

For her diligence in pursuing the quest for the artwork as a cover to adorn this book.

Elaine Franco

My wife since 1960, for editing this manuscript to make sure all is well.

Thank you all very much.

PREFACE

I used to think many years ago, there must be a key to answered prayer. If I could only discover what that key is, all of my prayers will be answered. I searched for what I thought might be the answer to all my problems.

One day I was reading Mark's Gospel, I don't know how many times I must have read it, but this time a verse that I must have read hundreds of times, stuck out to me. *Mark 4:11*, "And He said to them, 'to you it has been given to know the mystery of the Kingdom of God, but to those who are outside, all things come in parables'."

Here it was plainly written that there is a mystery, but, that we have been given the right to know it. From that day forward I embarked on a search to fully understand the mystery and my quest led me to *Mark 4:26-29*, "And He said, 'The kingdom of God is as if a man should scatter seed on the ground, and should sleep by night and rise by day, and the seed should sprout and grow, he himself does not know how. For the earth yields crops by itself: first the blade then the head, after that the full grain in the head. But when the grain ripens, immediately he puts in the sickle, because the harvest has come'."

If you study out Mark Chapter 4, Jesus is speaking about seed or seeds; He correlates seed to word. In your study you will conclude that words therefore, are the seeds that Jesus was speaking of. Especially God's Word or Words. When I speak God's Words over my life and ministry, they will surely come to pass. In *Romans 10:10*, it says, with the mouth confession is made to salvation.

As I began to confess God's Word over my life and over my body, I began to see changes. Now after many years of walking this way, I can boldly say I walk in divine health.

INTRODUCTION

"So you shall serve the Lord your GOD, and He will bless your bread and your water. And I will take sickness away from the midst of you." *Exodus 23:25*

"God is not a man, that He should lie, nor a son of man, that He should repent. Has He said, and will He not do it? Or has He spoken and will He not make it good?" *Numbers 23:19*

"For all the promises of GOD in HIM are yes, and in Him Amen, to the Glory of GOD through us." *II Corinthians 1:20*

Why do some not see it, or experience it for themselves? Why do some get healed and others don't? Is God a respecter of people? Is God showing partiality?

"For the wisdom that is from above is first pure, then peaceable, gentle, willing to yield, full of mercy and good fruits, without partiality and without hypocrisy." *James 3:17*

No, God does not show partiality nor does He decide who will get saved and who will not. He does not pick and choose who gets healed and who does not, WE DO!

"The Lord is not slack concerning His promise, as some count slackness, but is longsuffering towards us, not willing that any should perish but that all should come to repentance." *II Peter 3:9*

Since God does not want to see anyone perish, then why does He not just save them? Why doesn't He heal all that need healing? He has already said in His Word: "I call Heaven and earth as witnesses today against you, that I have set before you life and death, blessing and cursing; therefore, choose life that both you and your descendants may live." *Deuteronomy 30:19.* Then to make it perfectly clear to us, He said in *Proverbs 18:21*, "Death and life are in the power of the tongue, and those who love it will eat its fruit." *Romans 10:10* says; "For with the heart one *believes* to righteousness, and with the *mouth*, confession is made to *"salvation."* Salvation implies the ideas of safety, soundness, deliverance, healing and preservation. All-inclusive in salvation.

God decided when He made man to make him in His image, in His likeness, He gave us authority over all the earth and everything on it. In so doing He made man with a free will, Satan cannot violate your free will, and God will not violate it. What we do, what we say, is strictly our choice, God does not interfere. We see that in *Deuteronomy 30:19*, He told us to choose, however, since He is a loving Father, He suggests to us what the right choice would be.

In *Isaiah 53:4, 5* says, "Surely He has borne our griefs and carried our sorrows; yet we esteemed Him stricken, smitten by God, and afflicted. But He was wounded for our transgressions, He was bruised for our iniquities; the chastisement for our peace was upon Him, and by His stripes we are healed." In *1 Peter 2:24* it says, "Who Himself bore our sins in His own body on the tree, that we, having died to sin, might live for righteousness--by whose stripes you were healed." Isaiah looking <u>toward</u> the cross said, "we are healed," Peter looking <u>back</u> at the cross said, "we were healed." "We are" is past tense, implying that it has already been done. If you cannot see yourself as already being healed, there is a good possibility that you may never be healed.

Since God told us to choose life in *Deuteronomy 30:19*, and *Proverbs 18:21* tells us that life and death are in the power of the tongue, what we speak will determine our outcome! Some people will say when praying, "If it be Thy will Lord," we already know what His will is from *Isaiah 53:5* and *1 Peter 2:24*, adding "If it be Thy will Lord," that is a form of unbelief. When someone says, "If it be Thy will Lord," you can almost hear them say I don't believe what *Isaiah 53*, and *1 Peter 2* says.

Another hindrance to receiving what God has already provided for us, by His Grace, is expecting your healing some time in the future. God is the God of now, not the God of future. He told Moses to tell the children of Israel, "I Am who I Am," say to them, "I Am sent Me to you." Jesus told the Jews in *John 8:58*, "Before Abraham was, I AM."

When someone accepts Jesus as their Lord and Savior, we don't tell them to wait, they will get saved sooner or later.

15

Absolutely <u>not</u>! We tell them now that they have believed in their heart and confessed with their mouth that Jesus Christ is Lord, they have become a new creature, all things are new and all things are of God. We tell them that all of their sins are <u>now</u> forgiven never to be remembered again.

We tell them that they are now Sons or Daughters of Almighty God; and that was done (past tense) by their one act of faith in believing.

That holds true with healing, if you believe in your heart and speak with your mouth that by the stripes of Jesus you have been healed, then just like salvation always comes, nobody is ever denied salvation. In like manner, healing always comes, no one is ever denied healing. What happens next, just as the new believer has to now "fight the good fight of faith," so must the sick person, who accepted by grace, through faith what was provided by Calvary, must "Now fight the good fight of faith."

Most people think they want healing when in reality they are expecting a miracle. Healing is not instantaneous, you're not sick one moment and absolutely well the next. That would be called a miracle. Healing is a gradual happening. That's where the "fight of faith" comes in to play. First you believe that by the stripes of Jesus you have been healed, then you stand and keep standing on the Word of God. That is when confession comes into play, I speak with my mouth what I Believe in my heart. Your heart becomes fixed, firmly standing on what God, through His Word has said.

If at this moment, you cannot believe that by the stripes of Jesus you have already been healed, use this book as a tool, do not just read through it once and put it on the shelf to collect dust. Instead use it as a devotional every day, as you saturate yourself with the Word of God in it. You will become transformed in the renewing of your mind with the word of God and achieve success.

Table of Contents

BY THE STRIPES OF JESUS
I HAVE BEEN HEALED AND
MADE WHOLE. I AM NOT THE
SICK TRYING TO GET HEALED,
I AM THE HEALED, AND THE
ENEMY IS TRYING TO TAKE MY
HEALTH AWAY FROM ME.
I REFUSE THE CURSE,
INSTEAD I CHOOSE
BLESSINGS AND HEALING
AND HEALTH
IN JESUS NAME.

1

I PETER 2:24

"Who Himself bore our sins in His own Body on the tree, that we, having died to sin, might live for righteousness—by whose stripes you _were_ healed." _I Peter 2:24_

By the stripes of Jesus, I have been healed. To remain healed in spite of circumstances, I agree with the Word. The Word says I have been healed, not going to be healed someday. It is past tense, already done. Will I believe God's Word or will I believe the lying symptoms that are trying to attach to my body?

When Jesus was on earth He said, "If you can believe, all things are possible to him who believes," _Mark 9:23;_ will you believe you _are_ healed according to _I Peter 2:24_ or will you believe your body? Paul said in _I Corinthians 9:27_, "I discipline my body and bring it into subjection." Our bodies should not dominate us, instead we should dominate them. Bring them into subjection by the Word of God. That is a part of fighting the good fight of faith. The Word says, "You will declare a thing, and it will be established for you." _Job 22:28._ Decree that, by the stripes of Jesus you have been healed and you have been made whole.

A fruit of the Holy Spirit is faithfulness, remain faithful in your belief of what God's Word says. Don't allow your body to dominate and control what you believe, but stand firmly on _1 Peter 2:24,_ "By whose stripes you _were_ healed." Don't lose sight of it, keep the Word in your heart, meditate in and on it, get a vision of healing, see yourself healed not sick, and it will come to pass in your life.

I AM A WORLD OVERCOMER,

MY FAITH IS THE VICTORY THAT

OVERCOMES THE WORLD

I BELIEVE THAT

JESUS IS THE SON OF GOD

I AM BORN OF GOD

THAT MAKES ME A WORLD

OVERCOMER; THEREFORE,

I OVERCOME LYING SYMPTOMS,

THEY HAVE NO RIGHT TO ME,

NO POWER OVER ME.

I AM HEALED

BY THE STRIPES OF JESUS

2

I JOHN 5:4-5

"For whatever is born of God overcomes the world. And this is the victory that has overcome the world--our faith. Who is he who overcomes the world, but he who believes that Jesus is the Son of God? *I John 5:4-5*

We have resident in us, the victory that has already overcome the world. God has given to every man a measure of faith, that measure of faith according to the Apostle Peter is "like precious faith" that he had along with everyone else. According to John in *I John 5:4*, the faith that we received has already overcome the world. He says, "And this is the victory that has overcome the world." That makes us the believer, world overcomers. We don't have to try to achieve that, instead it has been given to us.

So as a world overcomer, we resist all of the onslaughts of the enemy and we overcome. In *Revelations 12:11*, we are told that we overcome the enemy by the blood of the Lamb and by the word of our testimony. That is, we testify as to what the Word of God says the Blood of Jesus has done for us. And we continually confess that we are overcomers. Our faith already is the victory that has overcome the world. We are not trying to get healed, we are already healed, and Satan keeps trying to take our health away from us. Don't let him! Stand on God's Word and it shall surely come to pass.

I HAVE BEEN <u>DELIVERED</u> OUT OF

THE POWER OF DARKNESS,

I NOW AM IN THE

KINGDOM OF GOD'S SON.

THERE IS NO SICKNESS IN THIS

KINGDOM, SO I REFUSE

SICKNESS AND DISEASE,

THEY HAVE NO AUTHORITY

HERE IN THIS KINGDOM.

I REFUSE TO GIVE THEM

PLACE HERE,

I AM THE

HEALED OF THE LORD.

3

COLOSSIANS 1:13
"Deliverance"

"He has delivered us from the power of darkness and translated us into the kingdom of the Son of His Love." *Colossians 1:13*

Before I accepted Jesus Christ as my Lord and Savior, I was under the control of the power of darkness. Satan, whether I knew it or not, was my lord. He had possession of me and I was under his domain. When I asked Jesus to become my Lord and my Savior, God the Father Delivered me out from that power of darkness and placed me in the Kingdom of His Son. Satan ceased from having any power over me. I was no longer his possession.

While in the kingdom of darkness Satan could put anything upon me he wanted to, but I am no longer in his kingdom, he has no access to me while I'm in the Kingdom of the Son of God. He has no right to me, no power over me. Now Jesus is my Lord and I receive from Him only. As long as I remain in His Kingdom and refuse any outside interference, it becomes impossible for me to ever be sick again.

God wants what His Will is in Heaven to also be done on earth. That is my endeavor, I choose the will of God in my life. There is no cancer in Heaven, there is no heart attacks in Heaven and there will be none in me. Thy Will be done Lord in my life, in my body and all that I am. I choose life, I choose blessing, and I reject the curse, in Jesus Name,

I PRESENT MY BODY TO GOD

AS A LIVING SACRIFICE.

I AM NOT MOVED BY WHAT I SEE,

NOR BY WHAT I FEEL,

NEITHER BY WHAT I HEAR.

I AM MOVED BY AND

STAND ON GOD'S HOLY

WRITTEN WORD THAT SAYS,

BY WHOSE STRIPES I HAVE

BEEN HEALED AND

MADE WHOLE; THEREFORE,

I AM HEALED AND

I HAVE BEEN MADE WHOLE.

4

ROMANS 12:1

A Living Sacrifice

"I beseech you therefore, brethren, by the mercies of God, that you present your bodies a living sacrifice, holy, acceptable to God, which is your reasonable service." *Romans 12:1*

We all want to please God by our service to and for Him. We have these lofty ideas on doing great exploits. Somehow we pass over what God calls reasonable service. Reasonable service is presenting our bodies to God as a living sacrifice.

What is a living sacrifice? It's when lying symptoms are attacking your body and you choose to believe God's Word above circumstances. Presenting your body to God by saying, "Father I am not moved by these lying symptoms, I am moved only by the Word of God." I therefore, present my body to you as a living sacrifice, I say my body is holy and acceptable to you, healed by the stripes of Jesus, redeemed by the Blood of Jesus, and useful for my Masters use.

Your Word says I am healed, I say I am healed, Your Word says, thanks be to God, who gives us the victory through our Lord Jesus Christ. I say thank you Father for giving me victory over these lying symptoms. I rejoice in your goodness and mercy and declare that by the stripes of Jesus I am healed and I have been made whole; therefore accept this, my body which I now present to you as a living sacrifice, Holy and acceptable to You Father as a living sacrifice, in Jesus Name, Amen.

I AM THE REDEEMED OF THE
LORD, WHOM THE LORD HAS
REDEEMED OUT OF THE
HAND OF MY ENEMY
BY HIS PRECIOUS BLOOD.
SICKNESS AND DISEASE
HAVE NO POWER OVER ME,
NO PLACE IN ME. THE
ENEMY MAY COME,
BUT HE HAS NOTHING IN ME.
I AM FREE, I AM FREE,
I AM FREE,
I AM REDEEMED!

5

PSALMS 107:2

Redeemed

"Let the redeemed of the Lord say so, Whom He has redeemed from the hand of the enemy." *Psalms 107:2*

We have not been redeemed by silver or gold, but by the precious Blood of Jesus. God paid a great price to deliver us out of Satan's hand and dominion. By saying so, I am agreeing with God that I have been redeemed. Everything that God has must be received. I receive what God, by grace, has given and provided for me by the words of my mouth. God is the one saying to say so. He is the one telling you to speak it out of your mouth.

"For with the heart one believes unto righteousness, and with the mouth confession is made to salvation." *Romans 10:10.* Redemption has brought us salvation, it has set us free. Whom the Son has set free is free indeed. If Satan is trying to put sickness on you say I refuse this in Jesus Name, I have been redeemed from sickness by the stripes of Jesus. By the Blood of my Lord Jesus Christ, I have been redeemed out of the hand of the enemy and by His stripes I have been healed.

The choice is yours, you are the captain of your ship, you decide which direction you will go, and it is determined by the words of your mouth, speaking God's Word only. As you speak His Word it will not return to Him void, but it will accomplish what it is intended to perform. Since I have been redeemed, I stay redeemed and sickness and disease cannot stay on me.

I HAVE BEEN MADE THE

RIGHTEOUSNESS OF GOD

IN CHRIST JESUS; THEREFORE,

I AM HOLY AND WITHOUT BLAME

BEFORE HIM IN LOVE.

I REFUSE TO FEAR, FEAR FINDS

NO PLACE IN ME, OPPRESSION

CANNOT COME UPON ME

BECAUSE I DO NOT FEAR.

GOD HAS NOT GIVEN ME

A SPIRIT OF FEAR, BUT OF POWER,

AND OF LOVE AND OF A SOUND
MIND; THEREFORE,

I HAVE A SOUND MIND

AND I DO NOT FEAR.

6

ISAIAH 54:14

"In righteousness you shall be established; you shall be far from oppression, for you shall not fear, and from terror, for it shall not come near you." *Isaiah 54:14*

In *Acts 10:38*, we are told that Jesus healed "all who were oppressed by the devil," the Holy Spirit through the author called sickness and disease 'oppression.' When the enemy tries to attack your body it is called oppression. How do we ward off sickness and disease (oppression); by refusing to fear. If you will not fear, refuse to fear, stay in faith, firmly planted on God's Word, then oppression cannot attach itself to your body. You shall be far from that oppression because you do not fear.

You must guard your heart and your mind from fear. Fear will kill you. By meditating on what God has already said, fear will have no entrance to you. Why would you fear when God already said, "By His stripes ye were healed," and "I am Jehovah Rapha, the God that healeth thee."

Besides all that, God's Word says that He, God, "has not given us a spirit of fear, but of Power and of love and of a sound mind." Confess that scripture over yourself until fear is completely gone from you. Never remain in fear, and never allow fear to dominate your thought life, instead, saturate yourself with what God has said, speak that out of your mouth, meditate on that until all fear is gone and your faith will bring you victory.

CHRIST HAS REDEEMED ME
FROM THE CURSE. INSTEAD
OF THE CURSE, THE BLESSING
OF ABRAHAM IS ON ME.
I AM BLESSED WITH FAITHFUL
ABRAHAM. JESUS BORE THE
CURSE FOR ME, THEREFORE,
I AM BLESSED, I AM BLESSED,
I AM BLESSED.
THE BLESSING ITSELF
OPERATES IN MY LIFE
AND OVERSHADOWS ME.

7

GALATIANS 3:13-14

"Christ has redeemed us from the curse of the law, having become a curse for us (for it is written, 'Cursed is everyone who hangs on a tree'), that the blessing of Abraham might come upon the gentiles in Christ Jesus, that we might receive the promise of the Spirit through faith." *Galatians 3:13-14*

We have been redeemed from the curse. In *Deuteronomy 28*, all of the curse is listed, none of it are we any longer subject to. Since I am redeemed, why would I allow the curse to come upon me? I am the captain of my ship. I decide who and what comes aboard my ship. What I allow is allowed, what I decide I don't want cannot come aboard my ship. I choose, I decide!

I choose instead of sickness and disease to allow the blessing of Abraham to board my ship. Life and death are in the power of the tongue, therefore, I believe it in my heart and I speak it with my mouth. I choose Life, I choose blessing. I declare and I decree that the blessing of Abraham is upon me. I am blessed, I am blessed and I am blessed.

In *Mark 11:24*, Jesus said, I can have what I say, therefore, I say and speak only blessing. I refuse to speak the curse. No matter what I am feeling or going through, I refuse to let it come out of my mouth. I only speak words that God can operate on.

MANY ARE THE AFLICTIONS OF

THE RIGHTEOUS, BUT THE

LORD GOD ALMIGHTY

DELIVERS ME OUT OF THEM ALL.

GOD IS FOR ME, NOT

AGAINST ME. SINCE

HE HAS GIVEN ME JESUS,

WILL HE NOT ALSO

GIVE ME ALL THINGS.

YES HE WILL.

I TAKE THEM BY FAITH

IN THE WORD OF GOD,

AND THEY ARE MINE.

8

PSALMS 34:19

"Many are the afflictions of the righteous, but the Lord delivers him out of them all. *Psalms 34:19*

Jesus said in *John 16:33*, "In the world you will have tribulation; but be of good cheer, I have overcome the world." We are now citizens of heaven. However, we still live on planet earth. Afflictions and tribulation may still come knocking at your door. Don't let them in! Jesus said be of good cheer.

We are told in *Ephesians 5:20*, to give thanks to God always in all things in the Name of Jesus. So, when afflictions of tribulation come at you, begin to thank God, cheerfully, for another opportunity to prove God's Word is true, and that Jesus has overcome the world for you. Believe it is true. Jesus said, "If you can believe, all things are possible to him who believe." Begin to confess with your mouth that Jesus has overcome the world for you, and that you are no longer subject to affliction and tribulations.

In *Isaiah 54:15*, it says, "Indeed they shall surely assemble, but not because of Me," saith the Lord. God is not your problem, God is your answer. As you refuse to accept afflictions and tribulations, and confess God's Word over them, they will gradually diminish until they are totally gone, Praise God.

THE GLORY WHICH
THE FATHER
GAVE TO
JESUS, HAS BEEN
GIVEN TO ME
BY MY LORD
JESUS CHRIST.
I AM NOW
ONE WITH GOD.

9

John 17:22-23

"And the glory which You gave Me I have given them, that they may be one just as We are one: I in them, and You in Me: that they may be made perfect in one, and that the world may know that You have sent Me." *John 17:22-23*

I either believe God's Word or don't believe it. There is no gray area. Therefore, I believe the glory that the Father gave to Jesus has been given to me by Jesus. Therefore, I am one with Christ Jesus. As one with the Lord Jesus Christ, I have all that he represents. He took all of humanities sickness, disease and infirmities upon His Body as my substitute, in my stead. He destroyed the power of sin, sickness and disease once and for all, for me and anyone else who dares to believe it.

I became a believer when I was born again. As a believer I choose to believe God's Word over anything else. Why would I choose to believe anything different but God's Word? Why would I speak out of my mouth anything different than what God's Word Says about me? Why would I look in a mirror and go away forgetting what I looked like? Doesn't God's Word say that looking at the Holy Written Word of God is like looking into a mirror and seeing yourself in it? So when I read, "By whose stripes ye were healed," I am seeing myself as if in a mirror and I see myself healed by the stripes of Jesus and I walk away speaking it out of my mouth, not what is attacking me. I choose to speak God's Word instead. Praise be to God!

I HAVE BEEN CRUCIFIED

WITH CHRIST,

MY OLD MAN, THE

OLD ME, DIED.

I AM DEAD TO

SIN AND ALIVE UNTO

RIGHTEOUSNESS.

HOWEVER, GOD THE

FATHER RAISED

ME UP TOGETHER WITH

CHRIST AND MADE ME TO

BE SEATED TOGETHER WITH

CHRIST IN HEAVENLY PLACES,

FAR ABOVE ALL PRINCIPALITIES

AND POWERS. THEREFORE,

SATAN IS NOW UNDER MY FEET.

10

ROMANS 6:7-8

"For He who has died has been freed from sin. Now if we died with Christ, we believe that we shall also live with Him."

You cannot make a dead man sick. I died with Christ and now Christ lives in me. As I speak these words over myself they become more and more real to me. My old man, that would be me before Christ, was crucified with Christ and died, so did I. In Ephesians Chapter 2, we are told that God made us alive together and raised us up together. If I did not die then I would not have to be raised. However, I did die and the life that I now live, in the flesh, I live by faith in the Son of God. I have been raised in His likeness.

As a raised being, the law of sin and death no longer have authority over me. The law of the spirit of life in Christ Jesus sets me free from the law of sin and death. Sickness is a preamble to death, I will not nor can I die sick. When I am finished accomplishing what God has called me to do, "God will take away my breath," *Psalms 104:29*, I will die and return to dust.

Because I was crucified with Christ (I died), sin now has no power over me, no authority over me, and the power of sin has been broken. Therefore, I can and I will walk in divine health. I reject the wages of sin which bring forth death, instead I receive the life of God, which is eternal life in Christ Jesus our Lord. I will never be sick another day in my life.

CHRIST HAS FORGIVEN
ALL OF MY INIQUITIES,
HE HAS HEALED ALL
OF MY DISEASES,
HE HAS REDEEMED MY
LIFE FROM DISTRUCTION,
THEREFORE, I CANNOT
BE DESTROYED.
HE NOW SATISFIES MY MOUTH
WITH GOOD THINGS SO MY
YOUTH IS NOW BEING
RENEWED ON A DAILY BASIS,
AS I SPEAK HIS WORD
OUT OF MY MOUTH.
THANK YOU JESUS

11

II TIMOTHY 2:15

"Be diligent to present yourself approved to God, a worker who does not need to be ashamed, rightly dividing the word of truth." *II Timothy 2:15*

Very few Christians understand the division in the Word of God, where it is found and where to place it to gain a better understanding of God's Word. The division is at the cross, what is before the cross and what is after the cross. Many things spoken of in the Old Testament is spoken to New Testament believers. For example: Psalms 103, forgiveness, healing and redemption is for us in the New Covenant. In the Old Covenant, sins were covered for a year by the blood of goats and bulls. That's why, when I confess Psalms 103, as I do almost every single day, I say it this way: v3. "He has forgiven all of my iniquities, He has healed all of my diseases;" v4. "He has redeemed my life from destruction, and He now crowns me with loving kindness and tender mercies." v5 "He now satisfies my mouth with good things, so that my youth is renewed like the eagles."

Once you begin to confess He has forgiven, He has healed, and He has redeemed me, you get a totally different mindset. You begin to think differently. You fight sin, sickness and disease immediately. You don't allow a little pain to remain in or on your body. You shout NO...I have been forgiven, I have been healed, and I have been redeemed!! You resist the onslaught of the enemy at every corner. You begin to think, "I'll never be sick another day in my life!"

I HAVE RECEIVED ABUNDANCE
OF GRACE, AND I HAVE BEEN
GIVEN THE GIFT OF
RIGHTEOUSNESS,
AS A RESULT,
I NOW REIGN IN THIS LIFE
AS A KING, THROUGH
CHRIST JESUS. THEREFORE,
I DO NOT ALLOW SIN,
SICKNESS, OR DISEASE TO
INHABIT MY BODY
IN JESUS NAME

12

ROMANS 5:17

"For if by the one man's offense death reigned through the one, much more those who receive abundance of grace and of the gift of righteousness will reign in life through the One, Jesus Christ." *Romans 5:17*

I have received not just grace, but the abundance of grace, that means more grace than I need and enough grace to cover all circumstances. And, if that were not enough, I was also given a gift, the gift of righteousness, not earned, not deserved, and not worked for.

An amplified definition of grace is, 'God's willingness to use His Power and His Ability on our behalf even though we don't deserve it. God's Grace is available to us to keep us in divine health, never to be sick again, we only play a small part in it. Our part, Believe!! Jesus said, "If you can believe, all things are possible to him who believes." "All Things" includes health, wholeness and soundness.

It has been recorded in God's Word that, "by the stripes of Jesus we have been healed." God said it, I believe it, and that settles it. Why would I ever allow my enemy to give me something that I do not want? No! Absolutely not! I refuse to allow anything that I do not want to be put on me.

With all this in mind (do not be conformed to this world, but be transformed by the renewing of your mind). I believe that I will never be sick another day in my life. By His Stripes, I am healed!!

NO EVIL SHALL BEFALL ME
NEITHER SHALL ANY
PLAGUE COME NEAR
MY HOUSE.
GOD HAS GIVEN HIS
ANGELS CHARGE OVER ME
TO KEEP ME IN ALL MY
WAYS, THEY BEAR ME
UP IN THEIR HANDS
LEST I DASH MY FOOT
AGAINST A STONE.

13

PSALMS 91:10

"No evil shall befall you, nor shall any plague come near your dwelling." *Psalms 91:10*

"All of the promises of God in Him are yes and in Him Amen, to the glory of God through us." God has promised that no evil shall befall us, and that no plague shall come near our dwelling. Yet, sometimes I think that some Christians open their front door and welcome sickness into their homes as a guest. It's almost as if they say, 'Welcome, we have been expecting you.'

No, a million times no, I declare and decree that no evil shall befall me and absolutely no plague comes near my house. I am the redeemed of the Lord, whom the Lord has redeemed out of the hand of the enemy, by His precious Blood.

When we stand on the promises of God and we refuse to be moved because they are yes, and they are amen. The Lord gets glory through us (*II Corinthians 1:20*). Jesus said, "Herein is my Father glorified that you bear much fruit." When you take God's Word, stand on it and allow it to come to pass in your life, you are bearing fruit. I chose to be a fruit bearing member of the Body of Christ, and refuse to allow sickness in my house or on my body.

Many believers talk more about what the enemy is doing instead of agreeing with what God has said, and with what has already been freely given to us. I choose life, I choose blessings in Jesus Name.

I DECLARE AND I DECREE
THAT I AM MORE THAN
A CONQUEROR
THROUGH HIM WHO LOVES ME.
I DECLARE AND I DECREE
THAT GOD IS NOW LEADING ME
IN A TRIUMPHANT PROCESSION
SHOWING ME OFF TO MY
ENEMIES, TELLING THEM
I AM OFF LIMITS
BY THE BLOOD OF THE LAMB
AND THE WORD OF
MY TESTIMONY.

14

ROMANS 8:37

"Yet in all these things we are more than conquerors through Him who loved us." *Romans 8:37*

"Now thanks be to God who always leads us in triumph in Christ, and through us diffuses the fragrance of His knowledge in every place." *II Corinthians 2:14*

God says that I am more than a conqueror through Jesus Christ, I say that I am more than a conqueror. God always leads me in triumph. God is ready to lead any of His children in a triumphant procession declaring to our enemy, 'My child believes My Word.' Since he believes My Word, declares it, and stands faithfully on it, his faith is the victory that overcomes you.

God is for me, not against me, since he already gave us Jesus, will He not with Him give us all things. He most certainly will. Everything God has must be received. Salvation must be received even though it has been freely given to all. Healing must be received, by steadfast faith, in God and His Word.

Since God says I am more than a conqueror, who am I to say that I am not. Since God is ready to lead us in a triumphant procession, who are we to refuse God! I choose to be more than a conqueror, I choose to allow God to lead me in triumph. I refuse the arm of the flesh, instead I choose divine providence. By His stripes I have been healed, that is my confession and I am not moving from it. That is what makes me more than a conqueror. Thanks be unto God.

GOD HAS DISARMED
PRINCIPALITIES AND POWERS
ON MY BEHALF,
HE HAS MADE A PUBLIC
SPECTACLE OUT OF
THEM, HE HAS TRIUMPHED
OVER THEM AND HAS
HANDED ME THAT TRIUMPH.
THEREFORE, I NOW
WALK TRIUMPHANTLY
OVER THEM.

15

COLOSSIANS 2:15

"Having disarmed principalities and powers, He made a public spectacle of them, triumphing over them in it." *Colossians 2:15*

Powers and principalities have been stripped of the armor they trusted in, Jesus fought and He won the battle, and He gave me His victory. Therefore, I already have the victory over my enemies. All they can do now is try and deceive me by telling me God does not love me. It's too late! I know that I am loved by God. I know that He loved me even when I was a sinner. Christ died for me. Now I am a son of the most high God and as long as I stay faithful to His Word, I cannot be deceived. If I am attacked in my body, I call it a <u>lying symptom</u>, because the truth is, "By His stripes I was healed."

Sickness is a fact, I don't deny it exists, I just refuse it to be in or on my body. Besides, truth (God's Word), always overcomes fact. By denying its existence does not let it go away. By choosing to believe what God has said and speaking it out of my mouth, brings me victory over <u>lying symptoms</u>. I am never sick, <u>lying symptoms</u> may be attacking my body, but I never give it place. Give no place to the devil. I even refuse to speak out of my mouth that <u>lying symptoms</u> are attacking me. Instead I choose life and I choose blessings and my speech is always in agreement with life and blessings; with health, healing, and wholeness. Praise the Name of the Lord.

THERE IS NOW
NO CONDEMNATION
TO ME BECAUSE I AM IN
CHRIST JESUS.
THE LAW OF THE
SPIRIT OF LIFE IN
CHRIST JESUS
HAS SET ME FREE
FROM THE LAW
OF SIN AND DEATH.
I CHOOSE LIFE,
I CHOOSE BLESSINGS,
I CANNOT BE DESTROYED
BECAUSE I WALK IN LOVE.

16

ROMANS 8:1-2

"There is therefore now no condemnation to those who are in Christ Jesus, who do not walk according to the flesh, but according to the Spirit. For the law of the Spirit of life in Christ Jesus has made me free from the law of sin and death." *Romans 8:1-2*

I refuse to walk in condemnation, there is no condemnation for me because I am in Christ Jesus. Before I made Jesus Christ my Lord and my Savior, I was in the power of darkness. Satan was my Lord and he controlled my life. When I accepted God's plan for salvation and received Jesus as my Lord and Savior, God the Father delivered me out of the power of darkness and translated me into the Kingdom of the Son of His love. Satan is no longer my lord, he has no place in me. I am now in the Kingdom of God's Son, who is now the Lord of my Life.

Satan has no right or authority to be in this New Kingdom where Jesus Christ is now Lord of my life. So if I spot just an inkling of his tactics, I immediately remind him, he is off limits. He can't be here, I resist him, and he must flee. Why would I accept anything from an alien? Besides, the Spirit of life in Christ Jesus has made me free from the law of sin and death.

I want you to notice in the law of the kingdom of darkness, you find death. In the law of the kingdom of the Son of His Love, you find life. God has already told us to choose life, why wouldn't we? Why do some fall for the lies of the enemy? As for me, me and my house will serve the Lord. We Choose life and blessings. Satan cannot and will not see me accept anything that he has!

I HAVE BEEN CRUCIFIED

WITH CHRIST

NOW CHRIST LIVES

IN ME AND THE LIFE

THAT I NOW LIVE,

I LIVE BY THE FAITH

OF GOD'S SON.

THEREFORE, I AM FREE

FROM THE PLOTS AND

PLANS OF THE ENEMY.

I NOW WALK IN TOTAL

FREEDOM.

I AM GOD'S

REDEEMED CHILD.

17

GALATIANS 2:20

"I have been crucified with Christ; it is no longer I who live, but Christ lives in me; and the life which I now live in the flesh I live by faith in the Son of God, who loved me and gave Himself for me." *Galatians 2:20*

I confess this scripture over myself daily and I claim it over myself; therefore, I can walk in its light. As a result, the life that I now live I live by faith in the Son of God. With faith in the Son of God, I am able to overcome any and all obstacles that come against me. Besides which, Christ now lives in me, whom shall I fear. If God be for me, who can be against me?

Jesus Christ ever liveth to make intercession for me, He gets all of His prayers answered. He sees things coming against me, being in me, before I see them. Greater protection cannot be obtained at any cost. So whom shall I fear, or whom shall I be afraid of? What name can be given to any attack that must not bow its knee to the Name of Jesus? We have here another reason not to ever give in to any plots, plans or devises of the enemy. Resist him strongly in the faith, the faith of God, which you have in you and the enemy will flee.

We overcome him by the Blood of the Lamb, and by the word of our testimony. When attacks come, resist them in the name of Jesus; lift up your hands and praise Him for another opportunity to prove His Word. Don't talk about the problem, instead praise God with the answer. Heaven and earth will pass away, but God's Word will abide forever.

FATHER, I AM ANXIOUS

FOR NOTHING,

BUT IN EVERYTHING

BY PRAYER

AND SUPPLICATION,

WITH THANKSGIVING,

I LET MY REQUEST

BE MADE KNOWN

TO GOD AND THE PEACE

OF GOD WHICH

SURPASSES ALL

UNDERSTANDING

GUARDS MY HEART

AND MIND THROUGH

CHRIST JESUS.

18

PHILLIPPIANS 4:6-7

"Be Anxious for Nothing, but in everything by prayer and supplication, with thanksgiving, let your request be made known to God; and the peace of God, which surpasses all understanding, will guard your hearts and minds through Christ Jesus." *Philippians 4:6-7*

This is not a suggestion, instead it's God commanding us not to be anxious. Anxiety brings a snare; it being the opposite of faith. Instead by prayer and supplication I remind God and myself, what His Word tells me. Then as I give thanks to God for meeting all my needs, according to His Holy written Word, what I am speaking out of my mouth, is what is in my heart in abundance. A peace then comes over me, reassuring me that what I believe in my heart, and speak with my mouth, will certainly come to pass.

Give no place to the devil by verbalizing, with your mouth, what the lying symptoms look like or feels like. Instead, confess God's Word; what you want, not what you don't want. As you do that, you will sense God's Peace overshadow you. When you sense His Peace, an assurance will come over you casting out all fear. Remember, "God has not given us a spirit of fear, but of power, and of love, and of a sound mind." I refuse to fear no matter how bleak the circumstances are, I absolutely refuse to fear. Fear has no power over me, and no place in me; instead, faith permeates my mind. Thy Word have I hid in my heart, that I may not sin against you.

GOD'S WORD IN MY
MOUTH IS AS FIRE,
AND IT IS LIKE A
HAMMER THAT
BREAKS THE ROCK
IN PIECES.
AS I SPEAK GOD'S
WORD TO THE
MOUNTAIN IT
SHALL SURELY
BE REMOVED.

19

JEREMIAH 23:29

"'Is not My Word like a fire?' says the Lord, 'And like a hammer that breaks the rock in pieces?'" *Jeremiah 23:29*

God's Word in my mouth is like a fire, and it is like a hammer that breaks the rock in pieces. If it needs to be burned out of my body or be broken into small pieces to exit my body, God's Word in my mouth will perform it. I have no excuses if sickness and disease remain in my body. I have been given authority to speak to the mountain. In *Isaiah* God says, "My Word shall not return to Me void, but it shall accomplish its intended purpose."

As Long as I remain faithful in speaking God's Word over my circumstances, as sure as heaven and earth will pass away, your condition must change. I read once that if you hit a rock with a sledge hammer, it begins to crack from the inside out. Therefore, after hitting the first blow, you will not see anything, as you continue to hit time and time again, the crack on the inside gets larger and larger; but, it is on the inside and you don't see a thing. That is how faith operates, the minute you begin to confess God's Word, the rock begins to crack on the inside. Therefore, don't quit; after having done all, stand!

As sure as the sun will rise again tomorrow morning, the rock will begin to crack and as you continue it shall come to pass. Has God not said this? Will He not do it? No Word of God is void of the power for it to come to pass. It most certainly will.

MY BODY IS A
TEMPLE OF THE
HOLY SPIRIT
WHO IS IN ME,
I AM NOT MY OWN.
THEREFORE, I
GUARD THIS TEMPLE,
I TAKE CHARGE
OF AND WATCH
OVER IT.
MY BODY IS A
SPECIMEN OF
PERFECT HEALTH.

20

I CORINTHIANS 6:19

"Do you not know that your body is the temple of the Holy Spirit who is in you, whom you have from God, and you are not your own?" *I Corinthians 6:19*

The Holy Spirit dwells in me, my body is His temple, I am not my own. As a result, it is my duty to guard over this temple, to be a good steward of what God has placed at my disposal. I have no right to allow a foreign entity to destroy my body. I am obligated to take charge of my body and preserve it blameless at the coming of our Lord Jesus Christ. We don't take God's Word seriously enough, we are not completely focused on the truth. Some pay more attention to lying symptoms than to God's Word.

Forever O Lord, Thy Word has been established in heaven. Heaven and earth will pass away but, God's Word will abide forever. Therefore, I will side with God's Word. I will put God's Word first place in my life. As I do that, God's Word will begin to work mightily in me. I consider not my body, as Abraham did, nor the symptoms that stare me in the face; instead, I become strong in my faith, all the while giving glory to God for His faithfulness.

In all things, not for all things, I give glory to God; I praise Him in it, not for the problem, but for the answer to my problem found in the Holy written Word of God. And, as I stand on His promises, they will surely come to pass.

I AM THE JUST,

I HAVE BEEN JUSTIFIED

BY THE BLOOD OF

THE LAMB, I HAVE

GOD'S ARMOR ON ME,

AND I STAND

AGAINST ALL THE

PLOTS, PLANS AND

SCHEMES OF THE

ENEMY. I AM

ALWAYS VICTORIOUS

THROUGH

JESUS CHRIST,

MY LORD AND SAVIOR.

21

EPHESIANS 6:11

"Put on the whole armor of God, that you may be able to stand against the wiles of the devil." *Ephesians 6:11*

We are told to put God's armor on; if I have God's armor on, then I look just like God. I am supposed to look just like God because I have been predestined to be conformed to His image, *Romans 8:29*.

The problem is that although we think we are people of faith, most of the time we speak faith but don't live it! Five times the Holy Spirit inspired writers of the Bible to record "the just shall live by faith."

In order to be in faith concerning *Ephesians 6:11*, I must believe that I have God's Armor on, even though I can't see it and I can't feel it. By faith I believe it's on, and because I have it on, the devil doesn't see me, instead he sees God.

Therefore, I am in a secret place of the most high God. I am abiding under the shadow of the almighty, so I am not moved by lying symptoms that may try to attach themselves to my body, I smile and say, "If you can't attack God, then you can't attack me, because I have God's armor on." That is one of the ways God has removed sickness from our midst.

GOD SENT HIS WORD

AND HE HEALED ME.

HE DELIVERS ME

OUT OF THE HAND

OF THE ENEMY,

BY HIS PRECIOUS

BLOOD I SAY I AM

THE REDEEMED OF

THE LORD,

WHOM THE LORD HAS

DELIVERED; THEREFORE,

I AM FREE FROM

SIN, SICKNESS,

AND DISEASE.

22

PSALMS 107:20

"He sent His Word and healed them, and delivered them from their destructions." *Psalms 107:20*

"In the beginning was the Word, and the Word became flesh and dwelt among us." The Word that God sent was Jesus. He came and said, "For this purpose the Son of God was manifested, that He might destroy the works of the devil." *I John 3:8*. And He did do it. We are told in *Colossians 2:15* that He, Jesus, has disarmed principalities and powers, and He made a public spectacle of them, triumphing over them in it.

He destroyed the power of our enemy for us. He took away the armor they trusted in, then He said, "All authority has been given to me," that would be one hundred percent authority. Since He has all authority, then our enemy has absolutely none. All he can do, if you let him, is deceive you into thinking he has some authority. He deceives you into thinking sickness; where, as children of Almighty God, we should be thinking healing. We are to cast down imaginations, that means don't imagine that you are sick, imagine you are healed. *Psalms 107:2* says, "Let the redeemed of the Lord say so, Whom He has redeemed from the hand of the enemy." He is telling us to say we have been redeemed; that is He has purchased us out of the enemy's hands by His precious Blood. Agree with God, don't agree with the enemy. Confess God's Word out of your mouth, get into agreement with God, not with your lying symptoms.

BY THIS MY
FATHER GOD IS
GLORIFIED, THAT I
BEAR MUCH FRUIT.
I REFUSE SICKNESS
AND DISEASE,
INSTEAD I CHOOSE
LIFE AND
I CHOOSE BLESSING,
I WILL BEAR MUCH
FRUIT BRINGING
GLORY TO GOD.

23

JOHN 15:8

"By this My Father is glorified, that you bear much fruit; so you will be My disciples." *John 15:8*

In order to bear fruit, you must start with a seed. Jesus already told us in the fourth chapter of *Mark*, "God's Word is seed." When I take the 'seed,' 'the Word of God;' such as *I Peter 2:24* and *Matthew 8:17*. Speak it forth out of my mouth, remain faithful to it and fight the good fight of faith. That 'seed' in time will germinate.

Jesus put it this way, "So is the kingdom of God, as if a man should scatter seed on the ground and should sleep by night and rise by day, and the seed should sprout and grow, he himself does not know how. For the earth yields crops by itself; first the blade, then the head, after that the full grain in the head. But when the grain ripens, immediately he puts in the sickle, because the harvest has come." *Mark 4:26-29*

Don't try to figure out how it is going to happen, the seed, God's Word, will produce a harvest. You can count on it! No Word of God is void of the power it needs to produce its harvest. Inherent inside God's Word exists God's power for that Word to reproduce itself. Your job or responsibility is to believe what you're saying is God's Word and God's Will for your life.

Jesus already bore on His own body every sickness known to mankind. The enemy has already been defeated and has no power or authority over you. Take charge, take control over your body, speak the Word, get fruit from it and bring honor and glory to Father. By this is the Father glorified, that you bear much fruit. Healing is fruit, glory to God.

GOD IS NOT
WITHHOLDING ANY
GOOD THING FROM
ME BECAUSE
I WALK UPRIGHT
BEFORE HIM
IN LOVE.
THEREFORE, I CAN
BOLDLY DECLARE
THAT BY THE
STRIPES OF JESUS
I HAVE BEEN
HEALED AND I HAVE
BEEN MADE WHOLE.

24

PSALMS 84:11

"For the Lord God is a sun and shield; The Lord will give grace and glory; No good thing will He withhold from those who walk uprightly." *Psalms 84:11*

Is healing a good thing? Then God promises to not hold back from us any good thing. So there remains one of two problems: number one is; do you believe it? Number two is; are you walking upright before Him? Remember, Jesus said, "If you can believe, all things are possible to Him who believes." So you need to check yourself and see if you really believe it or not. If not, work diligently to get to the place where you believe it. Do not be conformed to this world, but become transformed by renewing your mind with God's Word. Mutter healing verses and healing confessions to yourself all day long as much as possible. As you stay at it, the truth of the Word of God will begin to leave your mind and enter your spirit. Confession will bring possession.

Walking upright before God is an attitude of the heart. "With the heart man believes unto righteousness and with the mouth confession is made unto salvation." *Romans 10:10*. It is very important to remember that there is no condemnation to those who are in Christ Jesus. Why? Because the law of the Spirit of life in Christ Jesus has made me free from the law of sin and death. Therefore, with my heart and in the spirit, I now walk upright before my God. Before the foundation of the world, God chose me in Christ Jesus that I should be holy and without blame before Him in love.

JESUS IS THE VINE,
I AM A BRANCH
CONNECTED TO
THE VINE,
THEREFORE, I
RECEIVE MUCH
NOURISHMENT, AND
I PRODUCE MUCH
FRUIT THEREBY
BRINGING GLORY
TO MY HEAVENLY
FATHER. WITHOUT
JESUS I CAN DO
NOTHING.

25

JOHN 15:5

"I am the vine, you are the branches. He who abides in Me, and I in him, bears much fruit; for without Me you can do nothing." *John 15:5*

As long as I remain connected to the vine, I get all of the nourishment I need to stay alive, stay healthy and remain strong in the Lord. However, I must remain connected to the vine. In the beginning was the Word and the Word was God. Therefore, as I stay in the Word, I am connected to the vine. With the nourishment I receive I am now able to bear much fruit.

That is why God told Joshua, "This Book of the Law (the Word of God) shall not depart from your mouth, but you shall meditate in it day and night, that you may observe to do according to all that is written in it. For then you will make your way prosperous, and you will have good success." *Joshua 1:8*

To ask God to make your way prosperous and to give you success contradicts His Word. He said, "You will make your way prosperous and you will have good success." As I speak God's Word and meditate on it, (Not considering my body or lying symptoms), the Word that I speak and meditate on will germinate and grow and produce a great harvest for me. As I bear fruit, I will be bringing my Father glory. My body will also line up with the Word of God and the manifestation of my healing will appear. Abraham considered not his body, now dead, nor the deadness of Sarah's womb; instead, he was strong in faith giving glory to God. Taking into account what God had said, He is able to also perform.

I HAVE CONFIDENCE
IN GOD, I KNOW HE
HEARS ME WHEN
I PRAY ACCORDING
TO HIS WILL. SINCE
I KNOW HE HEARS
ME, THEN I KNOW
THAT I HAVE WHAT
I HAVE ASKED FOR,
AS A RESULT, I AM
THE HEALED
OF THE LORD.

26

I JOHN 5:14-15

"Now this is the confidence that we have in Him, that if we ask anything according to His Will, He hears us. And if we know that He hears us, whatever we ask, we know that we have the petitions that we have asked of Him." *I John 5:14-15*

Is healing the Will of God? Yes, absolutely yes! There is much scripture in God's Word that says so. To name one; When the leper came to Jesus saying, "If you are willing, you can make me clean." Jesus touched him and said, "I am willing, be cleansed." And immediately his leprosy was cleansed. Once you get this knowledge of God's Word from your head to your heart, you will begin to walk in divine health.

Secondly, we must believe that when we ask God anything according to His Will, He hears us. We are told in *II Chronicles 16:9* that, "God's eyes go to and fro the whole earth, to show Himself strong on behalf of those whose heart is loyal to Him." You are loyal to God by keeping His Word. You cannot separate God from His Word, the two are one.

By standing on the Word of God, and not allowing yourself to be moved from it, nor be taken out of your mouth, you will prosper and have success in the things you hope for. Faith becomes the guarantee of that which you hope and believe God for. It (faith) becomes the evidence of what you cannot see, and by it, you will obtain a good report. As you fight the good fight of faith, you will become more than a conqueror through Jesus Christ our Lord and Savior.

God always hears prayer spoken in faith. For your prayer to be a prayer of faith, it must line up with the Word of God. So when you pray, pray the answer not the problem. Speak your faith, then act out your faith. Faith without works is dead.

I HAVE BEEN

MADE ALIVE

WITH CHRIST,

I AM NOW

SEATED IN

HEAVENLY PLACES

IN CHRIST JESUS

FAR ABOVE ALL

PRINCIPALITIES

AND POWER, SATAN

IS NOW UNDER

MY FEET.

27

EPHESIANS 2:4-6

"But God, Who is rich in mercy, because of His great love with which He loved us, even when we were dead in trespasses, made us alive together with Christ (by grace you have been saved), and raised us up together, and made us sit together in the heavenly places in Christ Jesus." *Ephesians 2:4-6*

I am alive together with Christ, His life is my life, what He is I am. I am an heir of God, and a joint heir with Christ. Everything He got I get. He can no longer see death, he conquered death once for all, and therefore, He conquered death for me. Sickness is a prelude to death, but I have overcome the world through Christ Jesus my Lord and Savior. I am now seated in Heavenly places in Christ Jesus. That places me far above all principalities and powers, putting Satan under my feet. Therefore, sickness cannot stay on me. I have been redeemed from it. The responsibility to walk in perfect health now rests on my shoulders. What I am believing, and what I am saying, determines what I am. God has already done His part, "By whose stripes ye were healed." Not going to be, but healed; past tense! I am responsible to believe that God's Word is the truth; not lying symptoms. I am responsible to speak according to the Word of God and not by what I see.

I am told in *II Corinthians 4:18*, "We do not look at the things which are seen," (sickness & disease), "but at the things which are not seen," (the Word of God). "For the things which are seen," (with our physical eyes), "are temporary," (subject to change), "but the things which are not seen are eternal," (cannot be changed). I am continually fighting the good fight of faith, and I am continually walking in Christ's Victory!

THE WEAPONS OF
MY WARFARE ARE
MIGHTY IN GOD TO
PULLING DOWN
OF STRONGHOLDS.
THEREFORE, I
CAST DOWN EVERY
IMAGINATION THAT
TRIES TO EXALT
ITSELF AGAINST
THE KNOWLEDGE
OF GOD. AND I
BRING EVERY
THOUGHT INTO
OBEDIENCE TO
CHRIST JESUS.

28

II CORINTHIANS 10:3-5

"For though we walk in the flesh, we do not war according to the flesh. For the weapons of our warfare are not carnal but mighty in God for pulling down strongholds, casting down arguments and every high thing that exalts itself against the knowledge of God, bringing every thought into captivity to the obedience of Christ." *II Corinthians 10:3-5*

If you keep talking about what the enemy is doing or trying to do to you, you create a stronghold within you. If you have created a stronghold within you, that stronghold must be pulled down for you to get victory in your body. The weapons of our warfare are mighty through God, (the Name of Jesus, and the Blood of Jesus; to name just two), and are part of our arsenal, but you must use them to be effective.

The Bible says that at the Name of Jesus, every knee must bow. The title that medical science has given to what ails you, is a name. That name must bow its knee to the Name of Jesus. Command it to go in Jesus Name. Plead the Blood of Jesus over your body and command it to be conformed to the Will of God; your body must obey. The Blood of Jesus has not lost its power!

Do not allow any thoughts to stay in your mind that contradicts God's Word. Cast them down, refuse to meditate on the plots, plans and devices of the enemy. Instead, the Word of God shall not depart out of your mouth, but instead, meditate on it day and night, as you do, you will observe to do it. Then you will have good success and prosper in the thing you believe for. If you can believe, all things are possible to him who believes. Heaven and earth will pass away, but God's word shall abide forever. Forever oh Lord, has Your Word been settled in heaven.

WHEN I LIE

DOWN I AM

NOT AFRAID,

I LIE DOWN

AND MY

SLEEP IS SWEET

BECAUSE

GOD GIVES ME,

HIS BELOVED

SWEET SLEEP.

29

PROVERBS 3:24

"When you lie down, you will not be afraid; yes, you will lie down and your sleep will be sweet." *Proverbs 3:24*

Sleep is a blessing from God to those who love Him. Sleep is very important for good health. In *Psalms 127:2*, we are told, "God gives his beloved sleep." While you are sleeping your body rejuvenates itself; many good things happen in your body. God designed this for your body. All of your cells in your brain and in your body are being completely repaired and toxins get cleansed in your body. Your immune system is at an all-time high. The better you sleep, the better you will function in the morning. God created your body and He knows how it functions.

At the time of this writing, I am 83 years old and I enjoy a good eight hours of sweet sleep. I didn't always sleep so well, but when I discovered *Proverbs 3:24,* and *Psalms 127:2*, I began to make it a confession every day. My confession is, "God gives me His beloved sweet sleep." There is no reason why any born again believer should have sleepless nights, when God gives His beloved sweet sleep. Not getting a good night's sleep can keep you from receiving the healing you need. Determine right now that as God's beloved, you are going to start enjoying sweet sleep. One way to achieve this is to fall asleep meditating on a verse of scripture from the Bible. *Proverbs 3:24* is a good starting place. Then go on to *I Peter 2:24,* and *Matthew 8:17.* There are many confessions in this book that you can make. *Proverbs 4:20-22* tells us to, "give attention to My Words, incline your ears to My sayings. Do not let them depart from your eyes; keep them in the midst of your heart; for they are life to those who find them and health to all their flesh."

I DWELL IN THE

SECRET PLACE OF THE

MOST HIGH GOD. I

ABIDE UNDER HIS SHADOW.

HE IS MY REFUGE, MY

FORTRESS AND MY GOD.

IN HIM AND ONLY IN HIM

I TRUST. HE HAS AND

HE WILL ALWAYS DELIVER

ME FROM MY ENEMY.

NO EVIL SHALL

BEFALL ME,

NO PLAGUE COMES

NEAR MY

DWELLING.

30

PSALMS 91:1-2

"He who dwells in the secret place of the Most High shall abide under the shadow of the Almighty. I will say of the Lord, 'He is my refuge and my fortress; my God, in Him I will trust.'" *Psalms 91:1-2*

Psalms 91 is the greatest source of inspiration to me, I read it out loud every single day. Not only does it inspire me, but it adds daily to my faith. After having read *Psalms 91,* I can't understand why anyone would allow sickness and disease to remain in or on their body. It (*Psalms 91*), is a very important part of my arsenal. It has become my weapon of choice. Since I am in a secret place, Satan can't find me, he does not know where I am. How can he possibly try to attack my body if he can't find me?

We are told in *Romans 12:2*, to no longer be conformed to this world, instead "to become transformed by the renewing of our mind." I guarantee if you will confess the entire *Psalms 91* out loud every day for one month, at the end of that time, you will think differently about your body and your faith towards healing will have grown exponentially. You will become strong in the Lord and in the power of His might. Yes, there is some work involved, however, it will surely be worth your while.

God becomes to you what you confess with your mouth. Remember, everything God has must be received. "For with the heart, one believes unto righteousness and with the mouth confession is made unto salvation." God said He has put blessings and cursing before you. However, he said, "Choose life that you may live." The choice is yours.

I AM EVERYTHING

GOD'S WORD

SAYS THAT I AM,

I CAN DO

EVERYTHING

GOD'S WORD SAYS

THAT I CAN DO,

I CAN BE

EVERYTHING

GOD'S WORD SAYS

THAT I CAN BE

IN JESUS NAME

AMEN

31

HERE ARE MORE REASONS WHY I WILL NEVER BE SICK ANOTHER DAY IN MY LIFE

1. I am a son of God.

   I John 3:2; Ephesians 1:5

2. God renews my strength.

   Isaiah 40:31; Psalms 103:5

3. God watches over His Word.

   Jeremiah 1:12

4. God is for me, not against me.

   Romans 8:31

5. All of God's promises are yes and Amen.

   I Corinthians 1:20

6. I am a citizen of heaven.

   Ephesians 2:19-20

7. I am a member of the household of God.

   Ephesians 2:19-20

8. God has given His angels charge over me.

Psalms 91:16

9. I have been predestined to be conformed to the image of Christ.

Romans 8:29

10. I shall declare a thing and it shall be established for me.

Job 22:28

11. I can do all things through Christ who strengthens me.

Philippians 4:13

12. I am complete in Jesus, who is the head over all things.

Colossians 2:10

13. The gates of hell will not and cannot prevail against me.

Matthew 16:18

14. Jesus came that I may have life and have it more abundantly.

John 10:10

15. Greater is He who is in me than he who is in the world.

I John 4:4

THIS BOOK IS INTENDED TO BE A TOOL THAT ONE CAN USE IF YOU NEED HEALING IN YOUR BODY. THERE ARE THIRTY-ONE SECTIONS IN IT, ONE FOR EACH DAY OF THE MONTH.

GO THROUGH IT ONCE A MONTH, SATURATE YOURSELF WITH GOD'S WORD, ALLOW IT TO PERMIATE YOUR MIND, SOUL AND SPIRIT UNTIL GOD'S WORD COMES OUT OF YOUR MOUTH WITH POWER.

IF YOU DO THIS FAITHFULLY, YOU WILL EXPERIENCE GOD'S HEALING POWER IN AND ON YOUR BODY.

TRIUMPHANTLY, YOU WILL PRAISE HIM AND GIVE GLORY TO HIS NAME.

FATHER, I AM FORGETTING

THOSE THINGS WHICH

ARE BEHIND, AND I AM

REACHING FORWARD

TOWARD THOSE THINGS

WHICH ARE AHEAD.

I NOW PRESS FORWARD

TOWARD THE GOAL

FOR THE PRIZE OF THE

UPWARD CALL

OF GOD

IN CHRIST JESUS.

Philippians 3:13-14

I WILL NOT BE DEFEATED
ANOTHER DAY IN MY LIFE, I AM
TOTALLY VICTORIOUS THROUGH
JESUS CHRIST, MY LORD AND
SAVIOR.

I AM AN HEIR OF GOD, I AM
A JOINT HEIR WITH CHRIST.
I AM ABRAHAM'S SEED.
THEREFORE, AN
HEIR TO THE PROMISES.

Romans 8:17

I AM NOT SLOTHFUL, BUT I
AM A FOLLOWER OF THEM
WHO, THROUGH FAITH
AND PATIENCE, INHERIT
THE PROMISES OF GOD.

Hebrews 6:12

AS THE ELECT OF GOD,

HOLY AND BELOVED, I PUT

ON TENDER MERCIES,

KINDNESS, HUMILITY,

MEEKNESS, LONGSUFFERING

AND COMPASSION. I WILL

BEAR WITH OTHERS

AND FORGIVE OTHERS,

EVEN AS CHRIST

HAS FORGIVEN ME.

I PUT ON LOVE WHICH

IS THE BOND OF

PERFECTION.

Colossians 3:12-13

LORD, THANK YOU FOR
THE GRACE BY WHICH I MAY
SERVE GOD ACCEPTABLY
WITH REVERENCE AND
GODLY FEAR.

Hebrews 12:28

LORD MY SOUL THIRSTS FOR
YOU, MY FLESH LONGS FOR
YOU, TO SEE YOUR POWER
AND YOUR GLORY.

Psalms 63:1-2

LORD, AS YOUR EYES RUN TO
AND FRO THROUGHOUT THE
WHOLE EARTH, SEEKING ONE
WHOSE HEART IS PERFECT
TOWARDS YOU, SEEK NO
FURTHER LORD, CHOOSE ME.

II Chronicles 16:9

GOD'S DIVINE POWER HAS
GIVEN TO ME ALL THINGS
THAT PERTAIN TO LIFE AND
GODLINESS THROUGH THE
KNOWLEDGE OF HIM, WHO HAS
CALLED ME BY GLORY AND
VIRTUE, BY WHICH HAS
BEEN GIVEN TO ME EXCEEDINGLY
GREAT AND PRECIOUS PROMISES
THAT THROUGH THESE I
HAVE BECOME A PARTAKER
OF HIS DIVINE NATURE
HAVING ESCAPED THE
CORRUPTION THAT IS IN THE
WORLD THROUGH LUST.

II Peter 1:3-4

I HUMBLE MYSELF, OH LORD,
UNDER YOUR MIGHTY HAND
SO THAT YOU CAN EXALT
ME IN DUE TIME.

I Peter 5:6

I AM LIGHT IN THIS WORLD.
THANK YOU FATHER THAT MY
LIGHT ALWAYS EXTINGUISHES
DARKNESS WHEREVER I
GO, WHATEVER I DO.

Matthew 5:14

THANK YOU FATHER THAT
YOU HAVE GIVEN ME
AN UNDIVIDED HEART
THAT I MAY FEAR
YOUR NAME.

Psalms 86:11

THANK YOU FATHER, THAT
EYE HAS NOT SEEN, NOR
EAR HEARD, NOR HAS IT
ENTERED INTO THE HEART
OF MAN THE THINGS WHICH
YOU FATHER, HAVE
PREPARED FOR ME BECAUSE
I LOVE YOU. BUT, YOU
HAVE AND YOU ARE
REVEALING THEM TO
ME THROUGH YOUR
HOLY SPIRIT. FOR THE
SPIRIT SEARCHES ALL
THINGS, YES, THE DEEP
THINGS OF GOD.

I Corinthians 2:9-10

I DECLARE AND DECREE THAT
I OVERCOME SATAN BY THE
BLOOD OF THE LAMB AND BY
THE WORD OF MY TESTIMONY.

Revelation 12:10-11

IN THE NAME OF JESUS, I CLOTHE
MYSELF WITH COMPASSION AS
GOD'S CHOSEN MAN, HOLY
AND DEARLY LOVED BY GOD.

Colossians 3:12

THANK YOU LORD, THAT YOU
ARE NOW STRETCHING OUT
YOUR HAND TO HEAL
THROUGH ME AND THAT
SIGNS AND WONDERS ARE BEING
DONE THROUGH YOUR HOLY
SERVANT JESUS.

Acts 4:30

FATHER, I AM ANXIOUS

FOR NOTHING BUT

IN EVERYTHING BY

PRAYER AND SUPPLICATION,

WITH THANKSGIVING,

I LET MY REQUESTS BE

MADE KNOWN TO

GOD. AND THE PEACE

OF GOD, WHICH SURPASSES

ALL UNDERSTANDING,

GUARDS MY HEART AND

MIND THROUGH

CHRIST JESUS.

Philippians 4:7

THE GLORY WHICH THE
FATHER GAVE TO JESUS,
HAS BEEN GIVEN TO ME
BY MY LORD JESUS CHRIST.
I AM NOW ONE WITH GOD.

John 17:21

MANY ARE THE
AFFLICTIONS OF THE
RIGHTEOUS, BUT YOU
LORD DELIVER ME OUT
OF THEM ALL.

Psalms 34:19

THANK YOU FATHER THAT
WHEN I CALL UPON YOU, YOU
ANSWER ME, AND YOU SHOW
ME GREAT AND MIGHTY THINGS
WHICH I HAVE NOT KNOWN.

Jeremiah 33:3

HEAVENLY FATHER, I
DECLARE AND DECREE
THAT YOUR GRACE
IS SUFFICIENT FOR ME
FOR YOUR STRENGTH
IS MADE PERFECT IN
WEAKNESS; THEREFORE,
MOST GLADLY I WILL
RATHER BOAST IN MY
INFIRMITIES, THAT THE
POWER OF CHRIST
MAY REST UPON ME.

II Corinthians 12:9-10

THANK YOU FATHER THAT
THE SAME SPIRIT THAT
RAISED JESUS FROM THE
DEAD DWELLS IN ME, AND
HE GIVES LIFE TO MY BODY.

Romans 8:11

THANK YOU FATHER THAT
I NOW KNOW THE THINGS
THAT HAVE BEEN FREELY
GIVEN TO ME BY YOU LORD.

I Corinthians 2:12

FATHER, I THANK YOU THAT
YOU ARE DIRECTING MY
HEART INTO THE LOVE
OF GOD, AND INTO THE
PATIENCE OF CHRIST

II Thessalonians 3:5

THE SPIRIT OF THE LORD
IS UPON ME, BECAUSE
HE HAS ANOINTED ME TO
PREACH THE GOSPEL TO
THE POOR; HE HAS SENT ME
TO HEAL THE BROKENHEARTED,
TO PREACH DELIVERENCE TO
THE CAPTIVES, AND RECOVERY
OF SIGHT TO THE BLIND,
TO SET AT LIBERTY THOSE
WHO ARE OPPRESSED;
TO PROCLAIM THE
ACCEPTABLE YEAR OF
THE LORD.

Luke 4:18

I AM AN HEIR OF GOD,
I AM A JOINT HEIR WITH
CHRIST, I AM ABRAHAM'S
SEED, THEREFORE, AN
HEIR TO THE PROMISES.
AN INHERITANCE HAS
BEEN GIVEN ME. I AM
AN AMBASSADOR OF
GOD; AS AN AMBASSADOR,
ALL OF HEAVENS
RESOURCES ARE
BEHIND ME.

I AM THE REDEEMED OF THE
LORD, WHOM THE LORD HAS

REDEEMED OUT OF THE HAND
OF THE EMEMY BY HIS PRECIOUS
BLOOD AND I AM SAYING SO.

MY BODY IS A PAIN-FREE ZONE
BECAUSE JESUS BORE MY
PAIN IN HIS BODY ON THE
TREE AS MY SUBSTITUTE.

GOD IS WITH ME, HE WILL
NOT FAIL OR FORSAKE ME,
THEREFORE, I AM STRONG
AND VERY COURAGEOUS.

I HAVE RECEIVED

ABUNDANCE

OF GRACE,

AND I HAVE

BEEN GIVEN

THE GIFT OF

RIGHTEOUSNESS,

THEREFORE,

I NOW REIGN IN

THIS LIFE AS A

KING THROUGH

CHRIST JESUS

MY LORD.

THE LORD HAS SET APART
FOR HIMSELF WHO IS GODLY;
THE LORD WILL HEAR
WHEN I CALL TO HIM.

Psalms 4:3

THANK YOU FATHER THAT
YOU ARE WORKING IN ME,
BOTH TO WILL AND TO DO
YOUR GOOD PLEASURE.

Philippians 2:13

LORD, LET ME NOT GROW
WEARY WHILE DOING GOOD,
FOR IN DUE SEASON, I SHALL
REAP IF I DO NOT
LOSE HEART.

Galatians 6:9

I HAVE BEEN MADE

ALIVE WITH CHRIST,

I HAVE BEEN MADE

TO BE SEATED

IN CHRIST JESUS,

FAR ABOVE ALL

PRINCIPALITIES

AND POWERS,

SATAN IS NOW

UNDER MY FEET.

FATHER, I PRAY THAT THY
WILL BE DONE ON EARTH,
AS IT IS IN HEAVEN.

THANK YOU FATHER, THAT THE
BLOOD OF JESUS CONTINUALLY
CLEANSES ME FROM SIN.

ALL OF THE PROMISES OF GOD
ARE YES AND AMEN; I'M STANDING
ON THOSE PROMISES AND THEY
ARE COMING TO PASS IN MY LIFE.

THANK YOU LORD, WHEN I CALL
ON YOU, YOU ANSWER ME,
AND YOU ARE SHOWING ME
GREAT AND MIGHTY THINGS
I HAVE NOT KNOWN.

FATHER, I PRAY THAT
I MAY KNOW HIM,
CHRIST JESUS, AND
THE POWER OF HIS
RESURRECTION,
AND THE FELLOWSHIP
OF HIS SUFFERINGS,
BEING CONFORMED
TO HIS DEATH, IF,
BY ANY MEANS, I
MAY ATTAIN TO THE
RESURRECTION
FROM THE DEAD
IN JESUS NAME.

Philippians 3:10-11

THE LOVE OF GOD HAS BEEN SHED
ABROAD IN MY HEART BY THE
HOLY GHOST WHICH HAS BEEN
GIVEN TO ME. THEREFORE, I
CHOOSE TO WALK IN LOVE AND
ALWAYS FORGIVE EVERYONE

Romans 5:5

GOD CHOSE ME IN CHRIST JESUS
BEFORE THE FOUNDATION OF
THE WORLD THAT I SHOULD BE
HOLY AND WITHOUT BLAME
BEFORE HIM IN LOVE.

Ephesians 1:4

John Franco is available for ministry in and outside of the church setting. We would be pleased to hear from you if this book has had an impact on your life.

You may order additional copies of this book by E-mail.

Contact information:

E-mail: jfranco529@yahoo.com

November thru May

John Franco
465 Riviera Boulevard West
Naples, Florida 34112
(239) 692-9784

June thru October

John Franco
4 Heywood Court
Brick, New Jersey 08724
(732) 903-6209